Relationship Blueprints

The Secrets to Lasting Love

Table of Contents

Chapter 1. Introduction

Discover the magic potion for timeless affection by delving into our Special Report: "Relationship Blueprints: The Secrets to Lasting Love". This report is your treasure map to a realm of absolute harmony, everlasting passion, and profound compatibility. Our pages are not simply filled with theory, but they unveil tried-and-true strategies, practical tips and comprehensive insights garnered from decades of expert observations in the world of love and relationships. This enlightening journey will lead you to the secrets of sustaining the spark that keeps love alive, and enables you to build a successful, fulfilling relationship that not only survives, but thrives against all odds. Just one read of this life-altering report could intrigue, inspire, and ignite a newfound sense of enthusiasm that could shape and transform your love life forever. Don't miss out, gift yourself these love-ensuring insights and set the course towards a love story that lasts a lifetime. Marriage counselors and relationship coaches, be warned - this Special Report may just give you a run for your money!

Chapter 2. Understanding Love: A Deep Dive

The intricacies of love have confounded philosophers, psychologists, and poets for centuries. Its complexities are as daunting as they are beautiful, wrapped in layers of emotion, passion, and connection. But why does love hold such sway over our hearts and minds? What components decide the potency of this profound emotion? And how can we leverage these elements to maintain a perpetual bond in our relationships? Let's dive deep into the fascinating pool of affection to find answers.

=== The Definition of Love

Indeed, love emerges as one intricate entity that is hard to articulate with mere words. Yet, various disciplines have attempted to understand and define it in their unique ways. The psychological perspective explains love as a cognitive-emotional state, characterized by intrusive and obsessive thoughts about the object of affection. Alternatively, sociologists regard love as a socially constructed phenomenon influenced by cultural variables. From a biological standpoint, it's a complex neurobiological process involving the brain's reward system. As diverse as these definitions are, they offer valuable insights into understanding the multidimensional nature of love.

=== The Components of Love

Psychologist Robert Sternberg, in his Triangular Theory of Love, illustrates three fundamental components - intimacy, passion, and decision/commitment. Each component serves as a cornerstone contributing to the quality and endurance of love.

Intimacy, as Sternberg presents, is the feeling of closeness, connectedness, and bondedness in love relationships. It's the prime ingredient for weaving the fabric of love and involves the desire to give and receive emotional support.

Passion is the drives leading to romance, physical attraction, sexual consummation, and related phenomena in love relationships. It's the spark that initially attracts two individuals and keeps the flame of desire burning.

The third cornerstone **Decision/Commitment**, in the short-term involves the decision that one loves another, and in the long-term, the commitment to maintain that love. This conscious choice stabilizes a relationship and safeguards it from transient emotional weather.

=== Love and the Brain

Biologically, love is far from a mere flight of fancy. It's a potent mix of complex brain chemistry involving neurotransmitters, hormones, and specific brain areas. The stage of passionate love is dominated by dopamine, the neurotransmitter associated with reward and pleasure. This is why new lovers often exhibit symptoms of obsessive-compulsive disorder about their partners. As well, the stress hormone cortisol elevates during this phase, leading to heightened alertness and possibly explaining those butterflies-in-the-stomach sensations.

However, as relationships mature, these hormone levels stabilize and oxytocin, the 'bonding hormone,' becomes pivotal. This hormone, released during physical touch and intimacy, helps form the deep bonds that allow love to endure.

=== How Love Evolves

As relationships progress, they tend to transition from passionate love to compassionate love. Passionate love is intense, filled with longing, and predominately present in the early stages of a relationship. As the feelings of novelty and intrigue associated with a new partner lessen, passionate love generally simmers down.

In contrast, compassionate love is characterized by mutual respect, affection, and companionship. As the relationship matures, partners start to value emotional intimacy, trust, and shared experiences, marking a transition from passionate to compassionate love.

=== Love Languages

To maintain any relationship, communication is key. Dr. Gary Chapman, in his pivotal book, "The Five Love Languages," describes how people have varied ways to communicate and comprehend love. These languages are: 'Words of Affirmation,' 'Acts of Service,' 'Receiving Gifts,' 'Quality Time,' and 'Physical Touch.' Recognizing and understanding your partner's love language is pivotal to ensure that your expressions of affection are effectively communicated and comprehended.

=== Navigating Love

Understanding love is challenging, and navigating it, even more so. It demands continual effort, patience, and forgiveness. Compassionate communication underpins a loving relationship, and active listening can rejuvenate the bond during troubled times. Never underestimate the power of expressing gratitude and appreciation for your partner, as these can work wonders to strengthen a relationship.

Bearing in mind the dynamic nature of human beings and hence, their relationships, it's important to realize that love, too, evolves. It takes different forms at different stages, and each stage presents its unique beauty and challenges. The real magic potion to timeless affection lies in embracing this growth, in understanding each other's love language, and in being willing to flex and adapt as both of you evolve.

In short, love is a complex, multidimensional, and dynamic experience. With a deeper understanding of its components, its relation with our brain, and the transitions it undergoes, you are better equipped to cultivate a vibrant love life, one that thrives in adversity and radiates joy in prosperity. As this exploration has shown, love isn't just a powerful emotion, but a profound commitment, a promise that two people make to endure together, whatever life brings their way.

Chapter 3. Surviving the Honeymoon Phase: The First Big Hurdle

While it's often accompanied by the exhilaration of new love, the 'Honeymoon Phase' is undoubtedly a critical period in a relationship's life. This phase is all about discovery and adaptation, as both partners are still in the process of getting to know each other and finding the comfortable middle ground that melds their distinct identities into a united 'we'.

3.1. Unraveling the Honeymoon Illusion

The Honeymoon Phase is characterized by an initial spark of attraction, an unending flow of affection, and an overwhelming sense of euphoria. However, the real challenge begins when everyday reality begins to interrupt this perfect bubble. The crucial task at hand is to maintain the love and affection while understanding that the relationship must evolve beyond the allure of the honeymoon period.

One of the first discoveries you'll make is that your partner is not perfect. We are all human, with strengths and weaknesses. Hence, it is vital to accept each other's flaws while continuing to build on the strengths. To maintain a lasting connection, one needs to see the reality beyond the illusion of perfect compatibility.

3.2. Striking the Right Balance

Balance is a key aspect of any successful relationship. Especially in this phase, finding the balance between spending time together and retaining your individuality can be a tricky navigation. It's essential to remember that you are a team, but at the same time, you're still individuals with your own interests and personalities.

Finding time for your personal hobbies, interests, and friendships outside of the relationship maintains your sense of self. Balancing 'me' time with 'us' time is a healthy way to keep your relationship grounded while still cherishing the special bond you share.

3.3. Communicating Effectively

Effective communication is the cornerstone of any relationship. By 'effective', we mean genuine, open, and empathetic communication. It's vital to remember that your partner is not a mind reader. So, be clear about your thoughts and emotions. And, listen attentively when your partner communicates their feelings. A relationship thrives when both partners feel heard and valued.

Equally important is constructive conflict management. Arguments are normal in any relation. The key lies in resolving the disagreements in a healthy and respectful manner. Avoid blame games, focus on the issue, not the person, and remember to approach the disagreements as a team.

3.4. Building Mutual Respect and Trust

Mutual respect and trust are fundamental to any long-term relationship. Respect your partner's feelings, thoughts, decisions, and differences. Trust, on the other hand, goes beyond faithfulness; it's also about reliability and emotional safety. Being dependable and providing a safe space for your partner to express themselves without judgment builds a deep-seated trust.

Moreover, trust also involves being true to your word. If you make a promise, ensure you keep it. Deliver on your commitments, no matter how small they may seem.

3.5. Normalizing Changes

Understand that the relationship will start to look different as the honeymoon phase fades. The intensity of emotions might diminish, routines may become mundane, and butterflies in the stomach might not flutter as often. This isn't necessarily a red flag. Rather, consider this as moving towards a more comfortable, stable, and mature phase in your relationship.

3.6. Continuing to Explore and Grow Together

Despite the shift away from the honeymoon phase, it's vital to continue discovering new things about each other and the world around you. Embark on new adventures, learn new skills together, or even have intellectual debates. This helps in keeping the excitement and connection alive.

Also, work on personal growth as well as collective growth. Support each other's aspirations and dreams. Share in each other's triumphs and failures. It's all about growing and evolving together.

In conclusion, surviving the honeymoon phase is about embracing and navigating this crucial transitional period together with understanding, love, and patience. It's about redefining your relationship in a new light while keeping the love and affection intact. Remember, it's not about winning or losing; it's about building a life that you both love and cherish. With this wisdom in mind, you'll not just survive the Honeymoon Phase, but turn it into a springboard for a more profound and enduring relationship.

Chapter 4. Communication: The Lifeline of Love

Communication, often hailed as the lifeline of love, beats at the very heart of any truly successful relationship. It provides a lifeline, casting connection in times of both tranquillity and tumult. Good communication becomes the compass that navigates the complex pathways of understanding, empathy, and shared growth within a relationship.

4.1. The Power of Words

Consider words as tools in the vast relationship toolbox. Like any tool, their impact depends on how we wield them. We must use words empathetically, considering their power to build bridges or build walls. Meaningful communication goes beyond mere words – it involves genuinely understanding and respecting your partner's feelings and perspectives.

Knowledge and understanding form the foundation of effective communication. If you understand your partner's likes, dislikes, fears, and desires, you can express your thoughts and feelings in a manner that fosters shared understanding and shared growth.

4.2. Non-Verbal Communication: The Silent Dialogue

Non-verbal communication often speaks volumes where words fall short. The way you look at your partner, your body language, and even your silence, all contribute to the message you convey. Learn to 'listen' to your partner's non-verbal cues -an encouraging nod, a reassuring touch, or a comforting hug can often mean more than any words.

4.3. Active Listening: The Heart of Understanding

Active listening is not just hearing; it's a full engagement process. It's about interpreting what's being said and sensing what's left unsaid. It's about suspending any form of judgement and placing yourself in the shoes of your partner, developing a profound understanding of their perspective.

Take the time to truly absorb what your partner communicates to you. Respond with empathy and without interruption. Reflect their words in your responses. By doing so, you're affirming your interest in their feelings and thoughts.

4.4. Communication Through Conflict: The Art of Peace

Conflict is inevitable in any relationship. The challenge lies not in avoiding conflict, but in handling it constructively. It's natural that disagreements arise. What determines the resilience of your relationship is your ability to counteract these disagreements with effective communication – it must ensure that both parties feel heard and acknowledged.

Always approach conflict from a solution perspective rather than a problem perspective. Identify and express your feelings without accusing or blaming your partner. Use 'I' statements instead of 'You' statements to avoid sounding accusatory.

4.5. Fostering Emotional Openness

Being emotionally open with your partner requires a certain level of vulnerability. It's about letting your guard down and sharing your deepest thoughts, fears, and dreams. Emotional openness is about authenticity, about being your true self with your partner.

This openness requires courage, but the rewards are substantial. It strengthens trust, encourages empathy, and deepens the intimacy within a relationship. Maintain a non-judgmental space where emotions can be freely shared. Validate your partner's feelings and remind them that they're not alone in their experiences.

4.6. Navigating Love Languages

Gary Chapman's Five Love Languages identifies the different ways people experience and express love: Words of Affirmation, Acts of Service, Gifts, Quality Time, and Physical Touch. Identifying and understanding your own and your partner's love languages can vastly improve communication in your relationship.

The key lies in comprehension and compromise. You may not share the same love language, but understanding your partner's primary language can help you express your love in ways they'll appreciate most, and vice versa.

4.7. Delivering Difficult Conversations

At times, communicating difficult emotions or topics is necessary. It's crucial to approach these with sensitivity, patience, and empathy. Deliver your message clearly and honestly, but be tactful. Remember that the aim is not to hurt your partner but to provide a foundation for mutual understanding and growth.

In conclusion, the magic of love is delicately entwined with the art of communication. It's not about agreeing all the time or never having a collision of opinion, it's about nurturing an environment of mutual understanding, acceptance, and shared growth through consistent, effective, and empathetic dialogue. Love, like any other significant journey, is about learning and growing together. The journey may not always be a smooth ride, but with the right tools of communication, it can certainly lead to a wonderful destination.

Chapter 5. The Power of Compromise: Finding Unique Solutions

Communication is the cornerstone of any successful relationship, but this goes beyond the mere exchange of words. Real communication extends to the ability to understand and interpret what isn't being explicitly said, as much as what is. This is the fabric that weaves understanding and affection in the long run. With this understanding comes the power to compromise, an often understated yet remarkably potent strength, that can make relationships resilient, vibrant, and enduring.

5.1. Understanding Compromise

Compromise is not about losing or winning. It is not about gaining the upper hand or giving up your wants and needs to your partner. Rather, it is about finding a middle-ground, where the needs, desires, and ambitions of both partners can co-exist and potentially even nourish each other. This is contrary to destructive relationships where one person's gain is another's loss.

Where there is love, there should exist a desire to understand the other's standpoint, even if it does not necessarily align with our own. A duality of perception does not mean an absence of love; in fact, it suggests an opportunity for increasing depth and intimacy through constructive conversation and the practical application of compromise.

Let's consider a simple example: Your partner loves dancing, while you might prefer a night watching movies. Instead of taking an aggressive stand – dancing always or movies always – you could work towards a plan that accommodates both. One weekend for a dance, the next for a movie marathon. This example, while simple, paints the way compromises in relationships need to work.

5.2. The Compromise Spectrum

Compromises can range from small to substantial, each carrying its weight and impact. The important aspect to focus on is the spirit and willingness to compromise, which in turn reinforces the love and respect between the partners.

Some compromises simply serve as temporary resolutions to evade a potential conflict, while others could be life-altering decisions that define the course of a relationship. The bottom line is, it is paramount to apply wisdom to gauge the nature of the compromise and adapt your response accordingly.

5.3. Compromise as a Lifeline

Compromise acts as a lifebuoy, providing a safety net that can prevent the sinking ship of your relationship. When you are ready and willing to compromise, you corroborate the fact that your partner's happiness matters as much as yours.

However, it's crucial to understand that compromise does not mean a complete surrender of your desires, ambitions, or dreams. It can be tempting to keep making compromises in an effort to maintain peace in a relationship. But if this concession ends up becoming a one-sided ordeal, it can potentially breed resentment or even lead to losing oneself in the relationship. That's why it's crucial to strike that delicate balance where compromise becomes a path to relationship enhancement rather than degradation.

5.4. The Role of Empathy

Developing the ability to empathize with your partner is key to successful compromises. Empathy allows one to understand and share the feelings of another; it helps in knowing their position, providing insights into why they might want a particular thing or act a particular way.

A couple that has a profound understanding of each other is less likely to clash when interests divert, for they understand that everyone has their own individual needs and wants that need addressing. Empathy is like the magical glue that holds relationships together when they're threatened by the harsh winds of divergent interests.

5.5. Mastering the Art of Negotiation

Making compromises does not mean surrendering without contemplation. Successful compromises often involve negotiation. In any relationship, negotiation is a valuable skill, as it helps both partners reach a mutually beneficial resolution. As you master the art of negotiation, you learn how to present your viewpoint effectively and consider your partner's perspective as well.

Remember, the objective is not to win, but to find solutions that lead to harmony, understanding, and satisfaction. This is the realm where love thrives and relationships flourish, reinforcing commitment and understanding, assuring a future filled with affection, respect, and shared responsibilities.

Compromise is, indeed, an art and science in itself, one that needs mastering, especially if you wish to sustain love and affection in a relationship. Remember, each compromise builds a bridge that brings you closer, aids in celebrating differences, and promotes a bond that not just survives but thrives with time. So, cherish every moment of this journey to discover and learn, compromise and commit, grow and prosper in love. Keep in mind, every successful relationship has its fair share of compromises. It's the glue that turns two individuals into an inseparable unit, fluid and harmonious. It's the magic potion for timelessly thriving affection.

Remember the age-old proverb: 'It's better to bend a little, than to break a love affaire'. So in conclusion, cherish compromise as a strength, and witness the marvel it unfolds in your relationship!

Chapter 6. Keeping the Flame Alive: Revitalizing Passion in Long Term Relationships

During the initial stages of infatuation, it feels as if the spark of passion will never fade away, the intoxicating emotions will last forever. But as time passes and life's realities creep in, maintaining that level of passion becomes a challenge. It isn't that love diminishes, rather the intensity and fervor that characterized the early days of the relationship typically starts to wane. What follows then is the quest to revitalize this passion, to reignite that precious flame. This section delves into just that - we'll explore strategies, dissect concepts and ponder upon ideas that can help rekindle and sustain that flame.

6.1. The Value of Intentional Connection

One primary reason why passion tends to dwindle is a gradual decline in connection. Not merely physical connection, but emotional, intellectual, and spiritual connection as well. Intentional connection involves deliberately investing time and emotional energy in getting to know your partner's thoughts, feelings, and desires, and also sharing your own.

Strategy	Explanation
Conversational Connection	Regular and meaningful communication fosters understanding and emotional intimacy. Try to spend a few moments each day discussing non-routine matters, exploring each other's thoughts, feelings, aspirations and fears.
Quality Time	Spending quality time together allows you to build shared memories and experiences. These shared moments form the fabric of your relationship and fuel passion.
Conscious Presence	When interacting with your partner, practice being actively present. Minimize distractions and give full attention; this communicates respect and affection.

6.2. Deepening Emotional Intimacy

Emotional intimacy is the foundation of a lasting, passionate relationship. As you deepen your emotional bond, it reignites the romantic flame.

Strategy	Explanation
Vulnerability	Vulnerability is about opening up to your partner, sharing your deepest insecurities and fears facilitates deeper emotional connection.
Emotional Availability	Strive always to be emotionally available for your partner. This means acknowledging their feelings, providing support, and offering kindness and understanding in tough times.

Strategy	Explanation
Empathy	Empathy allows us to understand and share our partner's feelings. It's about seeing things from their perspective, which fosters intimacy.

6.3. Spicing Up Your Physical Intimacy

Although emotional connection is fundamental, physical intimacy also plays a crucial role in upholding passion, and it goes beyond sexual activities.

Strategy	Explanation
Physical Affection	Small gestures of physical affection like holding hands, hugging, or a peck on the cheek can keep the passion burning.
Mutual Satisfaction	Ensuring mutual satisfaction in the bedroom increases the bond between couples and revives passion.
Exploring New Frontiers	Introducing novelty in your physical relationship can generate excitement and reignite the spark.

6.4. Cultivating Shared Interests

Having shared interests encourages togetherness and creates opportunities for bonding over common pursuits.

Strategy	Explanation
Discovering Shared Passions	Having common hobbies or activities fosters unity and keeps the relationship vibrant.
Adventurous Escapades	Going on adventures together, doing something entirely new adds excitement to your relationship and makes shared memories.
Learning Together	Learning a new skill or acquiring knowledge about a common topic can stimulate intellectual connection and promote joint growth.

6.5. Practice Perennial Forgiveness

In long-term relationships, mistakes happen, and disagreements are inevitable. It's essential to cultivate a spirit of forgiveness.

Strategy	Explanation
Active Forgiveness	Cultivating the habit of active forgiveness helps to maintain harmony and keep the relationship from becoming suffocated by resentment.
Forgettable Memory	Once a matter has been settled, strive to forget it, without bringing it up in future disagreements. This alleviates recurrent emotional distress.

Keeping the flame of passion alive, especially in long-term relationships, requires ongoing effort, mutual respect and understanding, intentional connection, deep emotional intimacy, mutual satisfaction in physical intimacy, shared interests, and perennial forgiveness. These are viable strategies that, when implemented consistently, can help resuscitate a dwindling spark, revive passion, adding brightness to the flame of love between you and your partner. The reward of maintaining an enduring, passionate relationship is worth every ounce of the effort. Allow the flame to blaze bright and mighty, illuminating the pathway of your lifelong journey, making your love story one that isn't just enduring, but utterly fulfilling.

Chapter 7. Dealing with Fallout: Healthy Conflict Resolution

Ever heard the phrase, "Disagreements are inevitable, disharmony is a choice"? We all cope with disagreements in our own unique ways, yet the manner in which we navigate these troubled waters can make or break our relationships. Wise handling of disagreements fosters understanding, bolsters respect, and cultivates growth. On the flip side, poor handling can escalate minor disagreements into major conflicts and breed resentment, ushering in the cloud of disharmony. Let's peek into the mechanics of disagreements and acquaint ourselves with the best approaches to resolve them for a fully flourishing relationship.

7.1. Recognize Healthy Conflict

Before we dive headfirst into resolving conflicts, it's important to acknowledge that not all conflict is unhealthy or negative. Differences in opinion can stir up lively debates, reveal new perspectives, or promote personal growth. It allows room for communication enhancement and improving mutual understanding. Embrace disagreements, but make sure they contribute to the enrichment of your relationship rather than degrading it.

7.2. The Essence of Active Listening

Often we're so preoccupied with building our retaliation that we forget to listen. Listening isn't simply an auditory process; it requires our complete focus—our whole being. Active listening involves understanding your partner's point of view without pushing your own perspective. Nod and give verbal affirmations to reassure them.

Put aside your opinion momentarily to fully grasp theirs. This sincere interest demonstrates your willingness to understand and can reboot any conversation that's threatening to turn sour.

7.3. Employing Empathy

Conflict resolution becomes more manageable when we employ empathy. Walking a mile in your partner's shoes could offer a completely different viewpoint. Reiterate their viewpoint in your words to show that you understand their feelings and needs. By acknowledging their perspectives, you minimize the risk of any painful misunderstandings, laying the foundation for compassionate conflict resolution.

7.4. Speak Your Mind with I-Statements

We're often unconsciously offensive while expressing our aggravations. Rather than using accusatory "You-statements", practice "I-statements". For instance, instead of saying, "You never help with household chores," try saying, "I feel overwhelmed handling all the chores alone, and it would mean a lot if you could lend a hand." By stating your emotions and needs instead of blaming your partner, you reduce their defensiveness, keeping discussions peaceful.

7.5. The Art of Apologizing

While owning up to our mistakes is challenging, a genuine apology can mend feelings of hurt and resentment. An apology can prove you value your relationship more than your ego and displays commitment to avoid repeating the same mistakes. But remember, your words should match your actions. An empty apology will only add fuel to the fire.

7.6. Pause, Breathe, and Incorporate Breaks

As disagreements heat up, emotions may overrule logic. Sometimes, conflicts simply need a timeout. Take a break, breathe, and calm your emotions. You can resume the discussion when both parties are calmer and more composed.

7.7. Nurturing Patience and Flexibility

Patience and flexibility are two pivotal virtues empowering conflict resolution. Relationships aren't easy, and conflict resolution may take time. Extend your patience to your partner's reactions, and stay flexible in terms of possible solutions.

7.8. The Need for Healthy Boundaries

Establishing boundaries is essential to maintain a respectful environment. By clarifying what we find acceptable or unacceptable, we educate our partners on how to treat us. Ensure your boundaries cover all areas—physical, emotional, and digital—for a holistic approach.

7.9. Professional Help: Enlisting a Third Party

Various situations necessitate the intervention of an unbiased third party. Professional counselors can provide helpful insights and tools for both parties. They can assist with structured conversation guidelines, ensuring that both parties feel heard and respected.

The methods delineated are not merely about quelling the storm, but about transcending it to find new horizons of understanding, compassion, and mutual growth. Every conflict bears the potential for growth; it's all about our approach to resolution. Adopt these strategies, and you'll build not just a robust relationship but also enhance your personal mental and emotional acuity. Always remember, the strength of a relationship isn't measured by the lack of conflict, but how effectively and empathetically it's resolved. These strategies are not an exhaustive list, but they're compelling starting points that can transform how you perceive, approach, and resolve conflicts—guiding you to navigate the puzzling maze of disagreements with grace and effectiveness.

Chapter 8. Harnessing the Power of Empathy: Putting Yourself in Their Shoes

Empathy is a powerful tool, a silent connection that binds us together. It's an unwritten agreement to understand, to broaden one's perspective and step out of the confines of our own viewpoint. In the context of a romantic relationship, empathy becomes an even more potent bond, a bridge that spans the gap between two distinct individuals, joining them in a shared emotional landscape.

8.1. Fundamentals of Empathy

Though often considered an intangible concept, empathy is anything but. It is a skill that can be nurtured, developed, and refined with practice. But to do so requires an understanding of its fundamental components. Psychologists define empathy as the ability to relate to another person's feelings or thoughts as if they were your own. It is a profound ability to sense, understand, and connect to the emotions and mindset of another.

There are two types of empathy: cognitive and emotional. Cognitive empathy refers to understanding someone's thoughts, perceptions, and mental state. Emotional empathy, on the other hand, involves sharing the feelings of another person. In a relationship, it's not just enough to know what your partner is thinking; you need to feel what they're feeling.

8.2. Building Blocks of Empathic Communication

Communication is the cornerstone of any relationship. But not just any communication - empathic communication. This type of interaction involves not just speaking and listening, but understanding, acknowledging, and responding to your partner's emotions.

Practicing empathic listening ensures that you fully understand your partner's feelings and thoughts without judgement or criticism. This involves active listening, where you give your full attention to the speaker, and reflective listening, where you restate and reflect on what the speaker has said. Such a practice helps to make sure that you have a complete understanding of your partner's stance or feelings.

Another important element of empathic communication is expressing empathy. This is where you convey that you truly understand how the other person feels. Such expression could involve verbal affirmations, thoughtful gestures, or even just a comforting silence. It communicates to your partner that you acknowledge their feelings and share in their emotional experience.

8.3. The Power of Emotional Presence

Being emotionally present is more than just physically being there for your partner. It is about being attuned to and aware of your partner's emotions in each moment. It's about noticing their subtler feelings, those which might not be directly communicated. It's about understanding the unsaid, and reading between the lines to emotionally connect with your partner on a far deeper level.

There are times when the preoccupations of daily life may distract us from being emotionally present in our relationships. However, taking time to focus on your partner's emotional state can make a profound difference. If, for instance, they've had a difficult day, taking note of their expressions, responses, and body language can help you tune into their feelings.

8.4. Cultivating a Shared Emotional Experience

Sharing an emotional experience is more than just feeling the same emotions at the same time. It's about deepening your bond through shared experiences that evoke emotion and create mutual understanding. These can be as simple as watching a movie together, sharing a meal, or have in-depth discussions on a favorite shared topic.

Cultivating shared experiences promotes a sense of unity and helps you better understand your partner's reactions and emotional cues. Even challenging shared experiences, like overcoming a difficult situation together, can help to foster an even stronger emotional bond.

8.5. Empathy as a Relationship Fortifier

Every relationship encounters difficult times, and it is empathy that often acts as the great leveler. Empathy allows partners to ride the waves of disagreement, to understand each other, even when seeing eye-to-eye seems impossible. It is the key that unearths the underlying reasons and emotions, revealing the root cause of conflicts and thus paving the way for resolution and mutual growth.

The act of empathizing requires humility and even vulnerability, as it involves truly understanding and embracing another person's perspective. This can be particularly difficult in situations of disagreement. Yet it is in these situations that empathy becomes even more crucial.

8.6. Final Thoughts

Empathy is far from easy to cultivate. Many find it challenging, particularly in the context of a romantic relationship. However, by taking small steps each day, by nurturing open communication and active listening, by being emotionally present and nurturing shared experiences, you can develop the empathic bond that fuels lasting love.

The power of empathy lies in its transformative ability, in its capacity to cultivate stronger emotional connections, ensuring lasting, harmonious relationships. No magic potion guarantees timeless affection, but the careful cultivation of empathy in a relationship comes closest to alchemical magic in the world of love.

Chapter 9. The Secret Sauce: Habits of Long-standing Couples

We all have heard about couples who seem to just have it figured out, enjoying decades of love without seemingly tiring of one another. How do they keep the fire burning year after year? Let's break it down.

9.1. Understanding What Love Truly Means

Love is an emotional state, a combination of feelings that culminate in a deep affection for someone, making us act in ways that foster intimacy and connection. Here, we must differentiate between passionate love, which is characterized by intense emotions, sexual attraction, anxiety, and affiliation, and compassionate love, which is characterized by mutual respect, attachment, affection, and trust. Successful long-standing couples transition from a phase of passionate love to compassionate love, where passion is enriched with deeper feelings of attachment, security, and commitment.

9.2. Creating a Foundation of Trust

Successful relationships always carry a base layer of trust that withstands the test of time. Trust, in this context, means having confidence in your partner's intentions and behavior. It is built on a series of actions over time, and it's essential that efforts are made to maintain it. A breach of trust is often hard to recover from and can cause damage that is difficult to repair.

9.3. Open and Honest Communication

Without exception, enduring relationships flourish on open and honest communication. This is not limited to merely expressing positive things. It also encompasses discussing uncomfortable topics, disagreements, fears, and insecurities. Honesty fosters trust and intimacy, breaking walls and building bridges. Listening attentively and openly to your partner's point of view is also important.

9.4. Shared Goals and Values

Understanding what your partner values and prioritizing shared goals is a practice seen frequent among long-standing couples. Be it lifestyle, parenting, or finance; having shared values helps in navigating mutual decisions and facing adversities together. It is a potent glue that keeps couples bonded over time.

9.5. Spending Quality Time Together

Spending quality time strengthens the bond between couples. This does not necessarily mean always engaging in grand gestures or activities. Simple acts like preparing a meal together, taking a walk, or sitting down over a cup of tea for a heart-to-heart can equally facilitate bonding.

9.6. Embracing Individuality

Long-standing couples have mastered the art of maintaining individuality within the relationship. They respect each other's personal spaces, interests, and pursuits. These personal interests contribute to personal growth and satisfaction, which ultimately feeds into the health of the relationship.

9.7. The Power of Apology

Unwavering couples apologize and accept apologies. They understand that no one is perfect, and mistakes happen. Holding onto pride, grudges, or resentment can erode the relationship. The ability to sincerely apologize and forgive is vital to a long-lasting relationship.

9.8. Handling Conflicts Constructively

All couples experience conflict. However, successful couples handle conflicts in a basically positive way. They aim to resolve disagreements instead of winning the argument. They focus on the problem rather than attacking each other personally.

9.9. Unconditional Support

Supporting each other during times of crisis, distress, struggle, or change plays a big role in enduring relationships. When a partner feels deeply cared for during such times, it deepens the bond and builds a sense of security within the relationship.

9.10. Prioritizing Intimacy

Intimacy is not just about physical acts. It's about understanding and valuing each other's emotional needs. Connecting emotionally, understanding each other, and maintaining physical closeness contributes significantly to the longevity of relationships.

Each of these habits contributes to a strong relationship, building a stronger bond over time. However, it's essential to remember that successful relationships require constant work, patience, and dedication. There are little shortcuts. It may sound demanding, but once the value these habits bring to your relationship is witnessed firsthand, this unique recipe will become a natural part of your love life.

Chapter 10. Rekindling the Spark: Strategies for Difficult Times

Relationships, like the people in them, are living, evolving entities that require nourishment, nurturing and careful handling from time to time. The following content will provide insight into strategies, methods, and tools that can help rekindle the spark during difficult times.

10.1. Understanding the Nature of Challenges

In every relationship, challenges are inevitable. They stem from various sources - pressures from work, personal growth, financial stress, interpersonal conflicts, or health complications. Understanding the nature of these problems is the first critical step in tackling them. Instead of viewing these challenges as destructive elements, interpret them as opportunities for growth and improved understanding of each other. Remember, resilience stems from adversity.

10.2. Communication: A Vital Lifeline

The importance of open, honest, and compassionate communication cannot be overstated since it forms the backbone of any healthy relationship. When conflicts arise, confront them head-on through dialogue, avoiding resentment build-up. Always communicate your feelings accurately, empathetically, and without accusations. Practice active listening, giving your partner the space to voice their concerns without interruption. Don't focus solely on resolving the problem, but understand the emotions that they're experiencing.

A useful tool is the 'Emotion Wheel', where each spoke is a different emotional state. Identifying precisely where you and your partner reside on the wheel during a discussion can significantly enhance understanding.

10.3. Harnessing the Power of Patience

When disagreements occur, it's vital to practice patience. Allow your partner the time to process their feelings. Resist the urge to provide unsolicited advice or to try and 'fix' things instantly. The emphasis should be on empathetic understanding first and problem-solving later.

Draw on the wisdom of the '72 Hour Rule': Allow a cooling-off period after an argument. Post this, revisit the issue, and it might lead to constructive conversations rather than emotionally charged accusations.

10.4. Rebuilding Trust

When trust is shaken due to conflict or misunderstanding, rebuilding it requires time and effort. Avoid blaming and instead, take responsibility for your actions. Be honest about your feelings, and articulate your dedication towards rebuilding trust. Tangible actions like keeping promises and being consistent in your behavior will show your commitment.

10.5. Eye of the Storm: Crisis Management

Crises can be testing phases in a relationship, and managing them successfully requires a combination of communication, patience, and trust. Remember to focus on the enterprise – your relationship, rather than the individual troubles and faults.

A powerful tool called 'Crisis Map' can help visualize the crisis. Draw a diagram of the crisis, identify the central issue, and note the contributing factors around it. This exercise provides clarity and direction for the discussions.

10.6. Re-establishing Connection

Rekindling the spark involves finding shared moments of joy, tenderness, and connection. Be it through small acts of love, shared hobbies, or common goals, find that connection that ties you both together.

Insights from the 'Relationship Garden' metaphor could be enlightening. Consider your relationship akin to a garden, where love and affection are the seeds, and shared moments are the water and sunlight. Regularly nurturing and caring for this garden will promote its growth and bloom.

10.7. The Role of Professional Guidance

Professional help from certified therapists and counselors may be necessary for some situations. Online therapy platforms provide flexible options. While seeking help, remember there is no shame in it - rather it's a sign of strength and commitment towards betterment.

In conclusion, rekindling the spark during difficult times involves understanding the problem, communicating effectively, practicing patience, rebuilding trust, managing crises effectively, re-establishing connection, and seeking professional help when necessary. With these strategies in place, you can navigate the tides of tribulations and rekindle the romance, nurturing a lasting, soulful bond.

Chapter 11. Relationship Pitfalls: How to Avoid Common Mistakes

Every love story encounters hurdles along the path. Recognizing these common troubles could just be the first and most critical step to striving for a thriving, enduring relationship. The approach to circumventing these hindrances isn't always simple, but with some due diligence and conscious consideration, the journey to everlasting love is decidedly smoother and more rewarding.

11.1. Recognising Unrealistic Expectations

One of the first issues that often teeter the boat in relationships is the presence of unrealistic expectations. Ideally, it's most beneficial when partners can communicate their wants openly right from the beginning. Perfection doesn't exist, so expecting a partner to change their fundamental habits or personality traits as per one's convenience is a surefire way to invite resentment and dissatisfaction. It's more productive to foster acceptance, patience, and understand the concept of mutual growth.

11.2. Drawbacks of the Blame Game

Quite often, fights inflate into mammoth issues due to the blame game. It might feel momentarily rewarding to shift the responsibility for the dispute onto your partner's shoulders. However, this contributes to substantial long-term damage. The productive alternative is to concentrate on expressing your feelings and inviting an open discourse about your partner's viewpoint.

11.3. Miscommunication and Assumptions: A Dangerous Duo

Miscommunication breeds misunderstanding, while assumptions hinder open discussion about thoughts and feelings. These are two pivotal factors leading to relationship hurdles. The antidote involves clear, compassionate conversations allowing you to both express and understand each other's sentiment. This principle applies to both verbal and non-verbal communication, with heed paid to the latter, as it often speakers louder than words.

11.4. Promoting Positive Conflict Resolution

Even the strongest relationships encounter disagreement; it's an inevitable facet of two individuals navigating a mutual path. The difference arises in dealing with these conflicts. The secret lies in promoting constructive debates rather than destructive arguments. Couples who adopt a solution-focused attitude towards problems rather than targeting each other's frailties are the ones that blossom amidst adversities.

11.5. Keeping Emotional Accountancy at Bay

One profound yet often overlooked pitfall in relationships is the habit of keeping an emotional scorecard. It can be alluring to bring past flaws and arguments into current disputes, yet, this stokes the fire of resentment and hampers resolution efforts. The healthier approach would involve addressing issues as they arise and not letting them fester.

11.6. Nurturing Emotional Availability

Emotional unavailability can act as a major roadblock in relationships. The need to connect on an emotional level is inherent to humans, yet sometimes, fears or past traumas can inhibit this connection. Being open to your partner's emotional needs and making sure yours are recognised is the key to fostering mutual emotional availability.

11.7. Sidestepping Codependency

Another pitfall in relationships is codependency, where one person becomes excessively reliant on the other to satisfy their emotional and self-esteem requirements. This imbalanced relationship dynamic can be harmful to individual growth and the health of the relationship as a whole. For relationships to flourish, it is essential to foster independent identities and personal growth outside of the partnership.

11.8. Evading Complacency in Love

Indeed, comfortable love can feel like the best kind. However, complacency in relationships can lead to stagnation, diminishing the excitement and growth potential. Maintaining mutual respect, continuous learning about one another and promoting shared experiences can help keep the spark alive.

Addressing these common pitfalls can help pave the way for a healthier relationship. However, bearing in mind that no singular solution fits all - the applicability varies as per different couples' circumstances. Maintaining open channels of communication, practicing empathy, expressing gratitude, and maintaining respect are underlying principles that ensure the viability of relationships under various conditions.

Remember, sometimes experiencing these pitfalls could be necessary waypoints in refining your connection. They offer valuable lessons to grow individually and as a couple. So, let your love story thrive not despite, but because of its unique journey, navigating through these typical yet vital relationship struggles. Acknowledge them, confront them, learn from them, and let them guide you towards a love that, indeed, lasts a lifetime.

www.ingramcontent.com/pod-product-compliance
Lightning Source LLC
Chambersburg PA
CBHW071032260726
48661CB00007B/3008